ACKNOWLEDGMENTS

The photographs and paintings included in this book are reproduced by courtesy of the following:

Armitt Trust, page 14 *(above)*; Beatrix Potter Society, pages 5, 8 *(below)*; Ray Moller © Dorling Kindersley, page 27 *(below)*; Frederick Warne Archive, pages 13 *(above right)*, 20, 25 *(above)*; Bridgeman Art Library/Getty Images, pages 9 *(below)*, 17 *(below)*; Hulton Archive/Getty Images, page 11 *(below)*; Image Bank/Getty Images, page 25 *(below)*; Time & Life Pictures/Getty Images, page 19 *(below)*; National Trust, pages 18, 27 *(above)*; Private Collections, pages 6, 12, 17 *(above right)*, 24 *(below)*, 26; Victoria & Albert Museum, pages 8 *(above)*, 9 *(above)*, 10, 11 *(above)*, 13 *(above left)*, 14 *(below)*, 22, 27 *(centre)*

FREDERICK WARNE

Published by the Penguin Group
Penguin Books Ltd, 80 Strand, London WC2R 0RL, England
Penguin Putnam Inc., 375 Hudson Street, New York, New York 10014, USA
Penguin Books Australia Ltd, 250 Camberwell Road, Camberwell, Victoria 3124, Australia
Penguin Books Canada Ltd, 10 Alcorn Avenue, Toronto, Ontario, Canada M4V 3B2
Penguin Books India (P) Ltd, 11 Community Centre, Panchsheel Park, New Delhi 110 017, India
Penguin Books (NZ) Ltd, Cnr Rosedale and Airborne Roads, Albany, Auckland, New Zealand
Penguin Books (South Africa) (Pty) Ltd, P O Box 9, Parklands 2121, South Africa

Penguin Books Ltd, Registered Offices: 80 Strand, London WC2R 0RL, England

Web site at: www.peterrabbit.com

First published by Frederick Warne 2005
1 3 5 7 9 10 8 6 4 2

ISBN 0 7232 5689 6

Text by Nicola Baxter

Printed and bound in China

The
Story of
Beatrix
Potter

FREDERICK WARNE

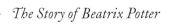

A SPECIAL RABBIT

O ne summer evening in 1893,
a young woman watched
luggage being loaded onto the night
train from London to Scotland.
She looked anxious. It wasn't the
trunks of clothes, fishing rods, or bulky
camera equipment that she was worried
about. It was a covered basket.
Inside the basket, a little
frightened by the noise,
was a rabbit called Peter.

Beatrix loved animals all her life. Here
she is with her rabbit, Benjamin Bounce

Peter Piper was the rabbit's name, and he went everywhere with the young woman. She even took him for walks on a lead.

No one on that busy station could have guessed that the young woman, Beatrix Potter, was going to become a world-famous author and illustrator of children's books. Or that the rabbit would become just as well known!

Beatrix Potter's most famous story is *The Tale of Peter Rabbit*.

All these well-loved characters were created by Beatrix Potter.

BEATRIX IS BORN

Beatrix Potter was born in London in 1866. She was the first child of wealthy parents who lived in a large house with several servants. Her father Rupert and mother Helen came from families in the north of England that had made money from cotton.

Rupert Potter took the photograph of his wife and daughter.

Beatrix and her little brother shared a love of animals.

Like most children of well-to-do families at the time, Beatrix spent her days in the nursery, looked after by a nanny. She did not often meet other children.

8

Beatrix painted these caterpillars when she was nine.

When Beatrix was six, her brother Bertram was born. Beatrix couldn't wait for him to be old enough to play with. Luckily, the children liked the same things and became good friends. They specially enjoyed the long family holidays that took place every year. Beatrix's lifelong love of nature and the countryside began on these holidays.

DID YOU KNOW?

When Beatrix was born, Queen Victoria was on the throne. Britain was a powerful country, with a huge empire.

FOUR-FOOTED FRIENDS

One of the interests Beatrix shared with her brother was a great love of animals. The family had a dog, called Spot, but the children often smuggled new pets up to their schoolroom. Many of these were wild animals, caught during holidays in the country. There were rabbits, mice, lizards, bats, birds, frogs, and even a snake, which soon escaped and was never seen again!

Beatrix loved Spot the spaniel.

Beatrix found this little lizard, Judy at the seaside and took her home.

When he was eleven, Bertram went to boarding school, whilst Beatrix was still taught at home.

A baby rabbit, painted when Beatrix was thirteen.

Beatrix was lonely, and poured out her feelings in a diary, written in code! The animals became her friends. She loved to draw them, and longed for lessons to end each day so she could spend time on her favourite hobby.

DID YOU KNOW?

In Victorian times, girls did not have as many choices as they do today. They were expected to get married and look after their husbands and families, or stay at home and take care of their parents.

A VERY FAMOUS LETTER

Beatrix with her father and brother.
Her beloved Spot was never far from her side.

When Beatrix was nineteen, her governess, Miss Carter, left to get married. This meant Beatrix could spend much more time drawing and painting.

Friends and family admired Beatrix's work. Her uncle suggested she sell some drawings, and Beatrix loved the idea of being more independent. She painted six Christmas cards showing a rabbit family, and the pictures were soon snapped up by a publisher. Beatrix longed to write and illustrate stories too, and was disappointed when her ideas were, at first, turned down.

Benjamin Bouncer was the model for Beatrix's Christmas cards.

Beatrix stayed in touch with Miss Carter, now Mrs Moore. In 1893, whilst on holiday in Scotland, she wrote to her friend's eldest child, Noel. "I don't know what to write to you, so I shall tell you a story about four little rabbits," she began.

Beatrix's letter to Noel. It became her inspiration for *The Tale of Peter Rabbit.*

DID YOU KNOW?

Luckily for Beatrix, drawing and painting were thought to be suitable hobbies for girls in Victorian times. She took drawing lessons, but often disagreed with her teachers!

BEATRIX'S FIRST BOOK

Over the next few years, Beatrix had much more freedom. She taught herself about fossils and fungi, and took up her father's hobby of photography. More of her drawings were sold and Beatrix enjoyed having some money of her own.

Beatrix became an expert on fungi and made detailed paintings of them.

Beatrix wrote her story with a picture opposite each paragraph.

She still liked sending story-letters to the Moore children, and in 1900 Mrs Moore encouraged her to try writing children's books again.

14

Beatrix made a longer story from the one about Peter Rabbit she had sent to Noel. She sent it to six publishers, who all turned it down.

Beatrix was a determined woman, and decided to pay for the story to be published herself. She found a printer and ordered 250 copies of *The Tale of Peter Rabbit*. They were so popular that she had to order more!

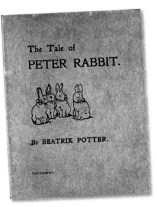

This is Beatrix's own printing of *The Tale of Peter Rabbit*.

DID YOU KNOW?

There were no computers when *The Tale of Peter Rabbit* was printed. Lead letters had to be put together by hand to form words and then made up into pages.

SUCCESS AT LAST!

Naughty Peter Rabbit quickly became a very well-known character.

W hile Beatrix was busy with Peter Rabbit, one of her friends was still trying to find a publisher for her. At last, a company called Frederick Warne & Co. agreed to take the book. It was a very good decision! All 8,000 copies of the first printing of *The Tale of Peter Rabbit* sold at once.

Beatrix took a great interest in what happened to her books, often visiting her publisher. Soon more books were agreed. *The Tailor of Gloucester* and *The Tale of Squirrel Nutkin* were next to appear.

Beatrix bought two squirrels to sketch for Squirrel Nutkin.

Beatrix was 36 when she became a successful author. At last the future seemed exciting, and not only because of her work. Beatrix's editor was a young man called Norman Warne. In 1905, Norman wrote to Beatrix and asked her to marry him.

Norman Warne was a gentle man, and very popular with his nieces and nephews.

DID YOU KNOW?

In Victorian times, a well-brought-up young woman always had a companion with her when she went visiting. Norman had never been alone with Beatrix when he asked her to marry him.

A SAD TIME

Beatrix wanted very much to marry Norman Warne, b her parents were not so keen. Perhaps they thought h wasn't the right sort of person, or perhaps they wanted her stay and look after them. Beatrix decided that at 38 she could make up her own mind!

This is Beatrix's own picture of Hill Top Farm, Sawrey, in the Lake District.

Beatrix had other plans too. With money earned from her books, she bought a small farm in the Lake District, havin fallen in love with the countryside during family holidays.

Beatrix worked on pictures for *The Tale of Mr. Jeremy Fisher* whilst at Sawrey.

Sadly, Beatrix's happiness did not last. A month after their engagement, Norman became ill and died. It was a dreadful time for Beatrix. She tried to cope with her sadness by throwing herself into her work.

We can see what the inside of Hill Top Farm was like from some of Beatrix's books.

DID YOU KNOW?

Norman's death was a shock, but illness and death at an early age were more common a hundred years ago. Many babies died before they were a year old.

19

SOMETHING FOR EVERYONE

B eatrix never forgot Norman, but work, friends and her love of the Lake District helped her to feel happy again. Her books became more and more popular. She was Frederick Warne's most important author.

Beatrix wanted children to enjoy her characters in other ways, too. She created a Peter Rabbit doll, painted Peter Rabbit wallpaper, drew pages for colouring books and even designed a Peter Rabbit board game!

Beatrix made the first Peter Rabbit doll herself. She put lead in his feet so he would stand up.

20

When she put a bear in *The Tale of Timmy Tiptoes*, Beatrix was careful to find out exactly how its fur should look.

Beatrix was always thinking about what her young readers would like. When she wrote *The Tale of Timmy Tiptoes*, she put in some animals specially for her American readers. There were grey American squirrels instead of red ones, a chipmunk, and even a bear!

Beatrix was very busy. She began to find it hard to find time for everything she wanted to do.

Beatrix even made fold-out books for very young children, like *The Story of Miss Moppet*.

BEATRIX THE FARMER

Beatrix wished that she could spend more time in the Lake District. She was becoming very interested in farming. A manager ran the farm for her, but Beatrix was keen to be involved. She wanted to keep Herdwick sheep because they were in danger of disappearing from the hillsides. Hill Top Farm also had cows, pigs, ducks and hens

Kep was Beatrix's favourite sheepdog.
She painted him looking after her Herdwick sheep.

Beatrix drew what she saw, and local people liked seeing their houses and shops in her books.

When Beatrix sketched her pigs in the pigsty, they would nibble her boots!

Beatrix's love for the Lake District grew and grew, and she could see that it might be spoilt if it was not protected.

Beatrix's little books were selling very well. With the money she earned, she bought more land and houses in the Lake District. She knew in her heart that she had found a home.

THE NATIONAL TRUST

Did you know?

In 1895 one of Beatrix's friends helped to set up what we now call the National Trust. It was started to help to save historic buildings and land. Beatrix was very interested from the beginning.

A HAPPY COUPLE

Beatrix's parents were now in their seventies. They spent part of the year in London and part in the Lake District. Beatrix worried about them . . . and they worried about what Beatrix wanted to do next!

Beatrix told a friend, "[This] is not a portrait of me and Mr Heelis. When I want to put William into a book – it will have to be as some very tall thin animal."

In 1912 William Heelis, a local solicitor, asked Beatrix to marry him. She had known and liked him for some time, but Beatrix's parents did not approve. Beatrix knew that she could decide for herself, but she wanted her parents to be happy, too.

Beatrix and Willie the day before their wedding.

Beatrix's brother Bertram had never told his parents that he himself had been married for eleven years! He decided to tell them now. Perhaps this made Beatrix's plans seem less shocking and her parents agreed to the marriage.

Beatrix became William's wife in October 1913.

Beatrix and Willie went to live in Castle Cottage, Sawrey.

DID YOU KNOW?

The year after Beatrix's marriage, the First World War began. Men and horses were needed for the war, and farmers had a difficult time.

A LIFE ON THE LAND

Beatrix was very happy with her husband. Although she loved to paint and draw, her farms and beloved Lake District began to take up most of her time.

After her father's death in 1914, Beatrix bought her mother a house near to her own in the Lake District. Mrs Potter lived there quite happily with four maids, two gardeners and a chauffeur to look after her!

Beatrix became a real countrywoman. She didn't mind if people talked about her shabby clothes or straight forward way of speaking. She was a familiar

Perhaps the most beautiful land that Beatrix bought was Troutbeck Park Farm.

26

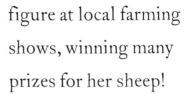

figure at local farming shows, winning many prizes for her sheep!

Beatrix's love of animals and children continued to the end of her life.

More than anything, Beatrix was keen to buy more land and houses, especially if they were in danger of being spoilt or pulled down. She soon owned thousands of hectares of land.

Greetings

Beatrix designed this card to support a children's charity.

DID YOU KNOW?

As electricity became more common, fewer people used candles or gas lamps. But Beatrix and Willie refused to have Castle Cottage modernised, which made it difficult for Beatrix to paint after dark.

REMEMBERING BEATRIX

As she grew older, Beatrix found that she could no longer walk in the hills she loved, but she had a painter's memory. "As I lie in bed," she wrote, "I can walk step by step on the fells seeing every stone and flower."

Beatrix died after a short illness at the end of 1943, aged 77. She had been a wealthy woman, and left fifteen farms to the Nation Trust, to be looked after as she had done. You can visi Hill Top Farm, which has been kept as she left it. Beatrix's stories are still

Beatrix loved the idea that her characters would appear in different ways.

28

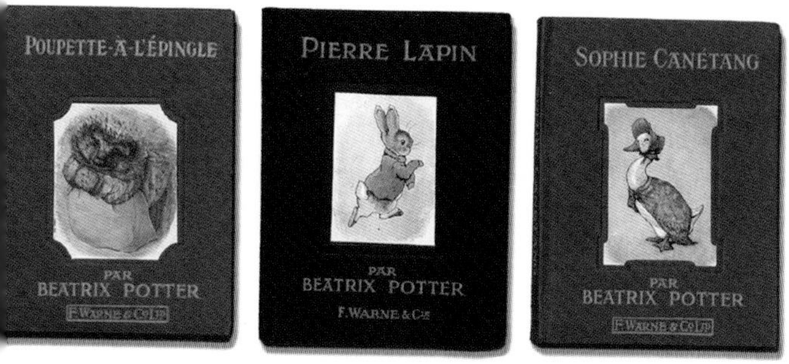
POUPETTE-À-L'ÉPINGLE
PAR
BEATRIX POTTER
F. WARNE & C° LTD
PIERRE LAPIN
PAR
BEATRIX POTTER
F. WARNE & C°
SOPHIE CANETANG
PAR
BEATRIX POTTER
F. WARNE & C° LTD

Beatrix's books are read all over the world in over thirty languages.

eing published all over the world, and are enjoyed by ew children every year. Peter Rabbit and some of the ther characters have appeared on everything from lippers to stamps. The company of Frederick Warne has one through many changes, but it still publishes eatrix's books and books about her – like this one!

s for Beatrix's characters, they seem as fresh nd lively as the day she painted them – and we re lucky enough to be able to love them as he did.

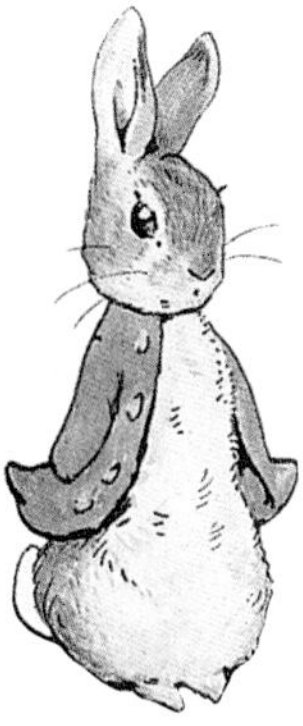